BIOGRAPHIES FOR KIDS

All about Martin Luther King Jr. Words That Changed America

Children's Biographies of Famous People Books

D1518780

BABY PROFESSOR

EDUCATION KIDS

Speedy Publishing LLC
40 E. Main St. #1156
Newark, DE 19711
www.speedypublishing.com

WHO WAS MARTIN LUTHER KING, JR.?

WHY IS HE FAMOUS?

WHAT DID HE DO TO BE FOREVER CARVED IN THE HEARTS OF THE PEOPLE?

Martin Luther King, Jr. was the second child of Martin Luther King, Sr. He was born on January 15, 1929 in Atlanta, Georgia.

He was a Baptist minister and a civil rights activist.
He played a very important role in American civil rights from the mid-1950s to 1968.

He admired advocates of nonviolence like Mahatma Gandhi. He dedicated his life to seek equality for African Americans and to end the segregation of African-Americans.

His devoted action led to the creation of the Civil Rights Act of 1964 and the Voting Rights Act of 1965. In 1964, he received the Nobel Peace Prize Award.

In his early years, he attended segregated public schools and he studied medicine and law at Morehouse College.

King earned his doctorate in systematic theology at Boston University.

In 1953, he married Coretta Scott, a young singer who studied at the New England Conservatory of Music. They had four children.

For less than a year,
the King family lived in
Montgomery. He became the
protest's leader and official
spokesman.

He and other civil rights activists founded the Southern Christian Leadership Conference (SCLC).

HAVE A DREAM

He became the president of this group. The group aimed to achieve full equality for African Americans through nonviolent movements.

Martin Luther King Jr. gave lectures against violent protests as he traveled across the country.

He also met with religious leaders, political leaders and activists. King, Jr. wrote the "Letter from Birmingham Jail", which was a civil rights manifesto.

It was an eloquent defense of civil disobedience for white clergymen who criticized him.

Martin Luther King Jr., together with civil rights and religious groups, organized the March on Washington.

This was a march for Jobs and Freedom. This was a peaceful political rally to protest the injustices towards African Americans.

The historical Washington March was attended by some 200,000 to 300,000 people and was regarded as a factor in the passage of the Civil Rights Act of 1964.

It was considered as the most important moment in the history of the American civil rights movement.

He delivered a very eloquent and famous speech, known as "I Have a Dream". This was a call for peace and equality. King, Jr. stood on the steps of the Lincoln Memorial as he delivered his most spirited speech.

He called for equality and peace. In his speech, he emphasized that all men were created equal. He was named the Man of the Year by TIME Magazine. While he was standing on the balcony of a motel in Memphis, on April 4, 1968, Martin Luther King Jr. was

assassinated. In 1983, President Ronald Reagan signed a bill in honor of Martin Luther King, Jr.

The commemoration of his death became a U.S. Federal holiday, which was first celebrated on the third Monday of January in 1986.

HAPPY MARTIN LUTHER KING DAY

18th JAN

MLK DAY

I have a dream...

King, Jr. was one of the most admired African-American leaders in history. He was a very eloquent man.

He was brave. He was nonviolent. He really had a dream for his people.

KIDS, DO YOU LIKE HIM?

ARE YOU ALSO WILLING TO STAND UP FOR WHAT YOU THINK IS RIGHT?

Visit

BABY PROFESSOR
EDUCATION KIDS

www.BabyProfessorBooks.com

to download Free Baby Professor eBooks
and view our catalog of new and exciting
Children's Books

CPSIA information can be obtained
at www.ICGtesting.com
Printed in the USA
LVOW05s1707080118
562242LV00005B/52/P